Coaching a
Student Teacher

Student Teaching: The Cooperating Teacher Series

This series is designed exclusively for cooperating teachers. We like to say, "These are the little instruction books that should have come with the student teacher!" The series acknowledges the cooperating teacher's important role in the student teaching experience and gives key guidance for effective supervision:

Book 1: *Preparing for a Student Teacher*
Book 2: *Coaching a Student Teacher*
Book 3: *Evaluating a Student Teacher*

The series is available as a set and as individual books so readers can explore the cooperating teacher role in totality or use the book that meets their current need. Each book offers essential techniques and practical advice. The user-friendly format provides a quick resource for the busy cooperating teacher to use in guiding the student teacher through a successful student teaching experience.

Coaching a Student Teacher

Marvin A. Henry and Ann Weber

ROWMAN & LITTLEFIELD
Lanham • Boulder • New York • London

Published by Rowman & Littlefield
A wholly owned subsidiary of The Rowman & Littlefield Publishing Group, Inc.
4501 Forbes Boulevard, Suite 200, Lanham, Maryland 20706
www.rowman.com

Unit A, Whitacre Mews, 26-34 Stannary Street, London SE11 4AB

British Library Cataloguing in Publication Information Available

Library of Congress Cataloging-in-Publication Data

Names: Henry, Marvin A., author. | Weber, Ann., author.
Title: Coaching a student teacher / Marvin A. Henry and Ann Weber.
Description: Lanham, Maryland : Rowman & Littlefield, [2016] | Series:
    Student teaching | Includes bibliographical references.
Identifiers: LCCN 2015041680 (print) | LCCN 2015049431 (ebook) | ISBN
    9781475824667 (pbk. : alk. paper) | ISBN 9781475824674 (Electronic)
Subjects: LCSH: Student teachers—Training of—United States. | Student
    teachers—Supervision of—United States. | Mentoring in education—United
    States.
Classification: LCC LB2157.U5 H46 2016 (print) | LCC LB2157.U5 (ebook) | DDC
    370.71/1—dc23

LC record available at http://lccn.loc.gov/2015041680

∞™ The paper used in this publication meets the minimum requirements of
American National Standard for Information Sciences—Permanence of Paper
for Printed Library Materials, ANSI/NISO Z39.48-1992.

Printed in the United States of America

Contents

Preface

This book is the second of a series of what we like to call "The little books that should come with your student teacher!" In our passion for the teaching profession, we have vowed to try to do something to better prepare cooperating teachers for the what-do-I-do-now moments in their supervisory role during student teaching.

You are the experienced practitioner in whose hands a student teacher has been placed. It is truly an honor! However, once the wave of excitement settles, you realize the immense responsibility for the development of your student teacher and consequently her future students and the teaching profession as a whole. Coaching a student teacher to the beginning teacher level requires a set of supervisory skills. This series is designed to concisely lay the foundation for your crucial role of shaping a future teacher.

In the first book of our series, we acquainted you with ways to prepare for the arrival of the student teacher and the guiding plan for the overall student-teaching experience. This second book centers on the important skills of observing, conferencing, and also supervising your student teacher's lesson plans and school-related experiences. We specifically chose the verb *coaching* for the title of this book because during the student-teaching experience, cooperating teachers actively coach through inspiration, demonstration, observation, analysis, and feedback. They persistently and generously give their time, expertise, and support to build a winning experience that prepares the student teacher for the reality of teaching.

Inside this book, you will find that research and experience are combined and illustrated with handy checklists and focused bulleted points.

There are to-do lists and forms to use. Each chapter also has a clipped "Notes to Self" for readers to jot their ideas regarding the topic. The size and set-up make each book a practical and useful companion.

Note our use of certain terminology in the book. We refer to the classroom instructor at the clinic school site as a *cooperating teacher* (CT). The candidate seeking a teaching degree is referred to as the *student teacher* (ST). The person who represents the university or college in a supervisory role is referred to as the *college supervisor* (CS). The use of pronouns that refer to men and women in these roles has been met by using "he" and "she" interchangeably.

Much of this series is generated from our full text, *Supervising Student Teachers the Professional Way*, seventh edition. You are encouraged to explore additional concepts and practical advice by reading more deeply in the expanded version, but for now, this series is a quick access to key points for your important cooperating teacher role.

We believe that every cooperating teacher has different needs based upon where she or he falls in the timeline of the student-teaching experience. Therefore, we have designed the three-volume series to focus on the following stages of the cooperating teacher role: the preparation, the coaching, and the evaluation. Cooperating teachers can use each book in the series as a guide for their current situation or use each to provide a heads-up for upcoming supervisory responsibilities.

We hope you enjoy the cooperating teacher journey as much as we have enjoyed preparing the map for you!

Ann Weber and Marvin Henry

Acknowledgments

Thank you to those heralded and unheralded cooperating teachers who supervise our future teachers.

Thank you to the countless classroom teachers, college supervisors, field directors, teacher educators, student teachers, publishing colleagues, and friends who inspired and helped us to pave the way for professional supervision of student teachers.

Thank you to our parents who heartened us throughout our lives and teaching endeavors.

Chapter 1

Should My Student Teacher Observe Others?

A colorful sports personality, Yogi Berra, is credited with the whimsical saying, "You can observe a lot by looking." This statement says what professionals know: observation is a valid, efficient, and beneficial way of learning. This is true for your student teachers too! Observing is a way of broadening awareness and understanding of styles, techniques, and results used by professionals.

The universality of requirements to view the cooperating teacher and various teachers during student teaching attests to the support that the teaching profession gives to this activity. Your student teacher should expect to make frequent observations as part of the total student teaching experience. The value of focused observations is multifaceted:

- *Exposure to variety.* Observation is a way of introducing student teachers to practitioners who possess differing skills and techniques and to different kinds of situations and students.
- *Effectiveness levels.* Observations provide the opportunity to see specific indicators of effective and ineffective teaching in action. This helps your student teacher see how personality factors, subject matter knowledge, and teaching techniques work together to bring about student learning and speculate about alternative strategies.
- *Self-discovery.* When your student teacher engages in self-analysis by viewing and analyzing a recording of himself in action, this allows him to assess his own teaching behaviors.
- *Teachers in action.* Student teaching may be the last opportunity to see other teachers in action. While collegial efforts are common in many schools, a substantial number of teachers still operate in isolation without professional dialogue or feedback from peers.

Observations of others can be active and exciting. A student teacher likely will have a positive attitude toward them when they provide answers to questions about teaching and learning. The challenge to the cooperating teacher is to provide productive and relevant viewing opportunities for student teachers. Yes, observations of other professionals are necessary in the development of your student teacher!

COOPERATING TEACHER'S ROLE

As the cooperating teacher, you will be involved both as a person being viewed and as one who is instrumental in scheduling and following up on observations of others. You facilitate the continued professional growth of student teachers by carefully guiding and discussing your student teacher's emerging perceptions of what it means to teach. A balance must be struck between the idealism of the student teacher, the theoretical influence of the college, and the reality of the real school environment. Observations help to broaden such perspective. *Watching* and *analyzing* are not the same thing. Without systematic guidance, student teachers may end up investing considerable amounts of time in an essentially unrewarding activity. Student teachers must be trained to observe as well as to teach (Treiber, 1984). The following stages outline your role in maximizing the observation opportunities for your student teacher.

Planning

The preparation involves determining what can be learned and who is to be observed. Over the student teaching experience, plan a variety of observations that considers the readiness, needs, and interests of your student teacher. Arrange times for different types of teaching situations, instructors, and settings.

Scheduling

The second step is to make arrangements for the visits. It is a matter of professional courtesy to request an observation in advance. Arrangements for observations may be made by you, your student teacher, or appropriate administrators. The student teacher should learn the procedure that is practiced at your school and follow that policy. Some schools operate on an informal basis while others have very specific procedures. There is a sample formal request on the next page.

Developing Purpose

The observations that are unappreciated are likely those where the student teacher has no idea of what to look for. A cooperating teacher helps structure observations so that they are considered to be meaningful and productive.

Once the visitation is arranged, clearly define the purpose for the chosen observation. A student teacher who realizes that it is important to note a teacher's questioning style, for example, will gain more from the experience than the one who is only instructed to "observe."

Determine appropriate methods to record the data to be used later for analysis. Data about the topic under investigation will provide the base for a follow-up conference. An analysis of the data then leads your student teacher in making decisions about future teaching and learning choices.

Do not overburden your student teacher with too many focus points during each observation. Narrow the focus to encourage your student teacher to look closely for data. Most prefer a single focus but some settings lend themselves to multiple focus points. There are an unlimited number of items from which to choose; the following is only a sampling.

Observation Request for Student Teacher

To:

From:

My student teacher, _____, will be observing various classrooms in order to collect data on teaching and learning. Data will be used for reflective purposes regarding his/her professional growth. As the cooperating teacher, I am seeking your approval for him/her to observe in your classroom. Your willingness to allow this observation in your classroom would be greatly appreciated!

Proposed Date(s):

Proposed Time(s):

Please sign and return this request form to the cooperating teacher.

☐ Observation in my classroom is approved. (Circle available dates and times above.)

☐ An alternative date and time is _____.

☐ I choose not to participate at this time.

Classroom Teacher's Signature: _____

Focus Points for Observations of Others:

- Classroom organization
- Classroom management
- Pupil relationships
- Teaching strategies
- Instructional materials
- Lesson content
- Lesson delivery
- Introduction and closure
- Student review
- Student questioning
- Student engagement
- Student motivation
- Accommodations
- Directions
- Assessment of students
- Objectives and standards

Observing Protocol

With notetaking materials in hand, your student teacher should arrive early enough to greet the host and allow time for any preliminary information that the classroom teacher desires to give. A student teacher can take more meaningful notes if he is aware of what is planned. Early arrival also ensures that the normal flow of activity will not be interrupted and helps the students adjust to a guest in the room.

The teacher and learners undoubtedly will take note of the visitor's reactions from time to time. Prompt your student teacher to display an active interest in the class and not appear to be bored or indifferent.

At the conclusion, your student teacher should leave the room quietly. The observer should then make a point to thank the teacher at the earliest convenience on the same day for allowing a visit to the classroom. The host teacher may want to make a few comments about the lesson or even solicit reactions to what was seen. A few positive comments by your student teacher are always in order.

Following-Up

The valuable observation experience finally concludes with an analysis session between you and your student teacher. This is invaluable in helping your student teacher interpret the data, contextualize the information that was gathered, and enables you to answer her questions. This discussion leads to a productive examination of teaching and learning.

Do not let the conversation be evaluative of the observed instructor. Use the recorded data and the student teacher's questions to direct the conversation and to encourage the student teacher to reflect on what was observed and applications to her own teaching. Your role is to listen as well as enlighten.

SEQUENCE OF OBSERVATIONS

Observations need to be sequenced throughout the entire period of student teaching. Early observations will focus on different ideas than later ones because your student teacher will have different professional needs and maturity level as time passes.

Initial Observations

In most cases the larger number of observations during the first few days of student teaching will be in the classroom of the cooperating teacher. Specific focal points for the observations are appropriately determined for the lesson or for the full day. You can use this occasion for modeling and for informing your student teacher about the nature of the class and its routine. These observations also allow your student teacher to get to know the learners and become aware of the classroom routine.

At different times during the initial weeks, you can schedule your student teacher to observe different focal points from the list on page 5. Choose the ones that will most help in the orientation of your student teacher. Remind your student teacher to focus on your behaviors as well as the dynamics existing within a classroom to help your student teacher to gain significant insights into the role he will soon be assuming.

The initial days are not too early for your student teacher to begin observing other teachers and other settings. It is beneficial to observe in and outside of his subject area and grade level. The early days also provide the time for him to see his students in other settings so that he can compare behavior patterns in the cooperating teacher's classroom with actions in other areas of the school.

Formative Observations

After the initial weeks of observations and after your student teacher experiences the role of teacher, new questions and needs will emerge about how to solve teaching problems and how to relate to students more effectively. Your student teacher may have specific questions which will help to determine the focal point of future observation. If not, you will sense a need and direct the observations.

These are popular areas for multiple observations of teachers and other instructional staff throughout the core of the student teaching experience:

- Effective teaching techniques. Focus on ways of arousing student interest, analyzing teaching behavior, and looking for ideas that would make a classroom successful.
- Better understanding of learners. Focus on words and actions that seem to influence student conduct, motivation, and understanding.
- Identification of teaching needs. Focus on identifying learner needs and ways which they are met.

Formative observations expand knowledge of teaching skills and learners. During this period, your student teacher analyzes his areas of strength and weakness while setting new instructional goals based in the analyzed data he gathered at the observations. As you continue to discuss observations with your student teacher, this dialogue causes him to reconstruct the experience and gain insights that he may have previously overlooked.

Summative Observations

This series of observations will be conducted near the end of student teaching. By this time the student teacher will have assumed significant teaching responsibilities. He will be viewing the teaching act in more abstract terms and be aware of its more subtle components. These final observations may be the most rewarding because your student teacher sees teaching in more scientific and artistic terms and has an increased awareness of the critical role of the teacher in directing learning. This sophisticated analysis of teaching through observation allows the student teacher to become more evaluative with the ability to detect relationships that have been overlooked earlier and to understand why a teacher is behaving in a particular way. In addition, the student teacher may be considering alternatives that will work or be adapted in his situation.

Purposeful observation allows the student teacher to have a valid frame of reference for the evaluation of teaching and a more comprehensive picture of the function of the school. If a student teacher fails to observe at any phase of the experience, a valuable learning opportunity is missed. Additionally, when observations are crammed into a brief period, a student teacher is denied an opportunity to learn as completely as possible. Your student teacher's notion of what to look for may be vague at all three levels of the experience so you provide insightful direction.

SCOPE OF OPPORTUNITIES

As explained, observations are not limited to you, your students, and your classroom. It is logical that expanding the scope of your student teacher's observations result in a broader, more sophisticated, and refined understanding of teaching practices and learning environments. The following are some ideas for observation settings.

Your School

Consider the scope of instructors within your school and school district. The variety of settings, content areas, grade levels, and teaching personalities offer multiple options for your student teacher to observe other educators whose classroom climates may differ from what they have been experiencing.

Other Schools

Significant perspective can be achieved through observations beyond the boundaries of the assigned school. Knowledge of other school and community settings help prepare your student teachers for placement in schools that may be unlike yours. Contact your professional colleagues to arrange for this type of opportunity.

Other Student Teachers

Observing veteran teachers is not the only option. As cooperating teacher, you can schedule time for your student teacher and another student teacher to observe each other and possibly provide feedback. Your student teacher will most likely have plenty to discuss with you afterward as well.

There is strong evidence supporting the use of peer observations as a learning activity for student teachers. Rauch and Whitaker (1999) find that pairs of student teachers improved their teaching by sitting in each other's classroom and giving written feedback. Student teachers also reported that the experience of being an evaluator was enlightening. Peer critiques, in addition to the feedback received from the cooperating teacher and the college supervisor, enhance the outcomes of the observation process (Giebelhaus, 1995).

Student teachers may be able to communicate with each other in more comprehensible ways because of their similarities. Hawkey (1995) suggest that student teachers may learn from each other because the intimidation factor is lessened when receiving a critique from a peer rather than a superior. Additionally, exposing student teachers to peer review is consistent with the expectations for licensed teachers and some professional organizations.

Self-Observation

A final recommended observation procedure is for you to arrange for your student teacher to view herself. The availability of technology has made self-analysis a practical reality. It is difficult to imagine a more striking way of illustrating and reinforcing concepts about teaching than by allowing a prospective teacher to observe herself as she is actively teaching. Visual recordings permit your student teacher to see both her weak and strong points and allow you to serve as a resource person in interpreting the behaviors. Although less dramatic, voice recorders are another possibility wherein student teachers can increase their knowledge about their own teaching through analysis (Anderson and Freiberg, 1995).

Technology recordings can be played more than once and, at times, are more convenient than coordinating an observation in real-time. You and your student teacher can view or listen to the recording at the same time or separately and then converse to analyze and set goals.

Self-analysis through technology is a technique worth considering. Use this list to remind your student teacher that:

☐ A recording cannot completely capture the essence of a classroom so the activity must be reviewed in context.

☐ In these days of slick presentations, the student teacher must be cautioned not to expect a perfect reproduction. Some of the sights and sounds on the monitor may be a distortion of what really happened in the classroom.

☐ Most schools have strict policies for recording students in the school setting and your student teacher will need to know them. Although the recording should be used strictly for student teacher analysis and then deleted, proper care must be taken not to violate any student privacy issues. You will want to emphatically remind your student teacher that nothing from the school setting should *ever* be posted on the internet.

An effective observation should result in improved student teaching performance. No student teacher ever became a skilled professional by simply watching masters apply the craft of teaching, but in well-designed observations, the student teacher becomes mentally engaged in the events as they unfold and uses that for improvement in his or her own future instructional choices. Thus, observations are as much a part of the student teaching experience as the work within the classroom.

Note to Self:
- ✓ A lesson plan is a ST's best teaching aid.
- ✓ Good lesson planning reduces stress & anxiety.
- ✓ Modeling, guidance, & feedback from the CT are essential.
- ✓ Lesson plan format, content development, & the submission policy vary.
- ✓
- ✓

Chapter 2

How Do I Supervise Lesson Planning?

A lesson plan is much more than notes on a paper. Learning the process of planning effective lessons is an evolving process for student teachers. Once they sat in college classrooms designing lesson plans for hypothetical students, but now they have a real context for each lesson and many real variables to consider.

As the cooperating teacher, you have the right to expect your student teacher to prepare both daily and long-range plans, but you may need to help him prepare, especially in the early phases of teaching. Guide your student through the planning process of *each* new content area and *each* new class of learners. Using the following sequence you can assist your student teacher in fully grasping the concept of lesson planning:

1. Verbalize your choices and decisions while demonstrating how you build lessons.
2. Co-plan lesson plans with your student teacher and then co-teach them.
3. Your student teacher independently plans lessons and gets feedback from you prior to teaching it.
4. Your student teacher moves toward building long-range plans.

As the cooperating teacher, you model and coach by providing examples of, and feedback for, well-developed lessons. You will witness the growth of your student teacher in the area of lesson planning as he gains experience and confidence in each of the content areas and with each set of students.

LESSON PLAN FORMAT

Cooperating teachers consider quality lesson plans to be essential to instruction, but according to S. F. O'Neal (1983), student teachers initially may not take planning seriously. Teacher education institutions require student teachers to write lesson plans. Your role is to monitor and support this requirement. Written lesson plans are a guide for the lesson as well as additional documentation of teaching, learning, and decision-making. Writing lesson plans is a habit that teachers are well-advised to develop.

If your student teacher needs some convincing that written lesson plans are important consider the following:

- Good plans reduce stress and anxiety.
- Planning helps ensure positive results from the lesson.
- Well-planned lessons can reduce student behavior problems.
- Planning lessens the amount of "ad lib" teaching.
- Well-planned lessons have a clear, purposeful instructional focus.
- Lesson plans show links to local, state, and national standards.
- Lesson plans are designed specifically for each group of students.
- Accommodations are documented in lesson plans.
- Written plans are a courtesy and security for a substitute.
- Most principals require and review written plans.

Your student teacher should be competent with various lesson plan formats learned in college courses, but you can also share your own and others used in your district. Having a variety of ways to structure lessons enhances the student teacher's ability to teach effectively.

The length of each written lesson plan will vary based on the complexity of the content, the amount of activities in the lesson, and the comfort zone of the student teacher. Often the student teacher moves from a detailed two-page lesson plan to a concise half-page plan with cue steps necessary to implement the lesson. The student teacher still thinks about the lesson in detail, but a long, written procedure may no longer be needed. Move your student teacher to this stage slowly after competency and confidence are demonstrated in each instructional setting.

RESOURCE AVAILABILITY

Cooperating teachers wonder whether it is proper to share lesson plans with their student teachers. Yes, sharing helps your student teacher to become familiar with your teaching style and to view models of effective plans. It may save time and frustration when she uses them as guides in writing her own.

On the other hand, handing over your lesson plans may imply that the student teacher should model the cooperating teacher. It may also prevent your student teacher from using fresh ideas from her college background and experience, particularly if it contrasts with your normal procedure.

An eclectic approach may be the best. A student teacher who is aware of a variety of ways to develop content in a lesson plan can then design plans that are most beneficial for her students' learning. Along with the teacher's manuals, there are scores of resource books and websites for every subject area where sample lesson plans can be easily accessed. Your student teacher brings ideas from her campus courses and now has access to examples of your plans. These all assist her in designing effective lesson plans

One final note about sharing your lesson plans with your student teacher is to also include information about available resources; knowing the items on this checklist will benefit her choices for lesson development:

- ☐ Materials within the classroom
- ☐ Media center materials
- ☐ Technology equipment
- ☐ Supplies within the school district
- ☐ Community sources

☐ Available funds

☐ Learners' profile and needs

☐ Publications

☐ Expertise of faculty members

FINE-TUNING

During the process of lesson planning, student teachers may forget details that contribute to the success of the lesson. After checking on content development, you can be proactive by directing him to fine-tune the following in his plans.

Technology

Although student teachers may be tech savvy, their background in using technology for teaching and learning purposes may be narrow. Research by Grove, Strudler, and Odell (2004) reveals that student teachers need help in learning how to effectively use technology in the classroom. You can provide insight for technology use by addressing the items on this checklist:

☐ Appropriate types of technology

☐ Presentational techniques

☐ Strategies for pupil engagement

☐ Classroom management

Diversity

There is a range of abilities and needs to be addressed in the typical classroom. Fleming and Baker (2002) find that more attention is given to diverse needs when detailed plans are used. Your student teacher will have ideas for addressing students' needs, but your experience makes you a valuable resource for identifying and providing ideas for the specific learners in your classroom.

Standards

Instruction is aligned with national, state, and local standards. Your student teacher may need initial assistance in defining and connecting the lesson's objectives, instruction, outcomes, and assessments to appropriate standards.

Classroom Management

Content cannot be addressed, technology cannot be used, student diversity cannot be recognized, and standards cannot be met if the student teacher does not have effective classroom management. You assist by nudging your student teacher to consider various strategies and to recognize areas of the lesson that might pose potential problems in her proposed lesson plan.

SUBMISSION OF PLANS

How far in advance should lesson plans be completed and submitted for review by the cooperating teacher? This is a frequent question and an arbitrary answer will not suffice because there are too many variables involved. Set realistic expectation by considering each situation, knowing that lesson plans should be prepared far enough in advance so that you can review each one and your student teacher has time to modify as needed.

Clarity for your student teacher's submission of his lesson plans means that you will:

- ☐ Provide a guideline for lesson plan formats.
- ☐ Give a specific deadline for submission of plans.
- ☐ Offer feedback as quickly as possible so alterations can be made.
- ☐ Teach lessons when your student teacher fails to submit an adequate lesson plan.

Early Weeks

It is frequently a problem for student teachers to submit plans very far in advance, especially in the early weeks of student teaching. At the beginning, most lesson plans are shared with the cooperating teacher one day ahead of instruction. Many choose to discuss the plan later that same day or at the start of the school day in which it is to be taught. Whatever time is chosen, it is wise to allow your student teacher plenty of time to revise the plan after your review.

As the Experience Advances

As your student teacher's experience advances and he more fully understands the content, the planning process, and the learners, he develops abilities for long-range planning. It is common for student teachers in the middle to late stage of the experience to submit weekly lesson plans. Unit plans are often completed and ready for feedback a week or two in advance of the unit's starting date.

Planning in advance is especially necessary when outside resources are to be used. Media and library specialists, for example, often cannot respond immediately to requests for materials. Make certain that your student teacher understands the necessary protocol to secure help from other professionals and support personnel.

Effective planning is the foundation for effective instruction. Learning to design lesson plans is a complex skill which takes time to evolve in your student teacher. Your modeling and coaching become a foundation for that crucial decision-making process.

Note to Self:

✓ Informal & regularly scheduled formal observations are necessary.

✓ Collect data during observations to later analyze with the ST.

✓ Analysis of observational data leads to improvements.

✓ Use a variety of observational methods & focus points over time.

✓

✓

Chapter 3

How Do I Effectively Observe My Student Teacher?

Your student teacher assumes more and more teaching responsibilities. You slowly fade from the front of the classroom into another important position, that of observer. This is *not* a passive role because you actively collect data while maintaining a low profile. You are keenly aware of what is planned to happen and now watch as things unfold. What you witness becomes the foundation for conversation with your student teacher in pursuit of advancing her professional skills.

Observation of your student teacher will occur in informal and formal ways. Both are important throughout the whole student teaching experience. Informal observations occur more often and through your casual notation of a situation. It is often followed by a quick-fix conversation with your student teacher.

Formal observations, on the other hand, occur several times a week and data is collected. Later, a conference occurs that centers on that data. The depth of conversation as a result of a formal observation is in contrast to the informal one because it is scheduled, has a specific focus on a topic or task, and includes a structured analysis.

The necessity of formal observation is obvious. Analysis and evaluation cannot be reliable unless you are aware of your student teacher's behaviors. Awareness comes through direct observation, in which the cooperating teacher assumes the role of a data collector. By collecting data and then later analyzing together, you coach your student teacher in becoming competent in analyzing her own teaching.

SETTING THE STAGE

While advantageous, being formally observed can be uncomfortable and intimidating. These practices may be useful in helping your student teacher feel more comfortable with an observer present:

- Remind your student teacher that you are collecting data to help her professional growth.
- Formally observe her on a regular basis so familiarity and routine are established.
- Observe from an unobtrusive location.
- Display positive nonverbal behaviors while writing and watching.
- Share your notes with your student teacher.
- Give at least one compliment soon after the observation.
- Follow up with a conference that includes analysis of the data collected.
- Reverse roles by inviting the student teacher to observe, collect data, and discuss your teaching.
- Avoid interrupting the student teacher while she is in front of the students.

An important note about interruptions: You retain ultimate responsibility for the care of your students while watching a novice work with your pupils. Your student teacher will probably make mistakes and it is tempting to interrupt the class. Some common temptations that might cause you to want to interrupt the flow of the class are as follows:

- Your student teacher makes an error in subject matter.
- You wish to add supplementary information.
- Your student teacher gets into difficulty and does not know how to overcome it.
- The students look to you for answers or information.
- You want to control the behavior of one or more pupils.

Unless asked to participate, your interventions may be disconcerting for a student teacher. Regardless of your good intentions, your student teacher may find it difficult to regain composure or continue the flow of the lesson after you have interrupted. Additionally, while your interruption may correct an immediate difficulty, it can initiate more serious problems, such as a deterioration of student respect by conveying the idea that your student teacher is merely responding to your directives.

Interruptions should occur only when irreversible damage is being done to the class. Most concerns can be discussed after class and then your student teacher can make the necessary adjustments in an ensuing session.

Formal observations should be scheduled regularly. It is not uncommon to conduct formal observations several times a week. Various topics and methods for the focus of the observation can be determined by you, your student teacher, or the college supervisor. Sharing the data and the follow-up conference outcomes is valued by the college supervisor.

IDENTIFYING DATA TO COLLECT AND ANALYZE

Formal observations and their analysis advance your student teacher. The data from your observations become the foundation for conferencing and, therefore, the professional growth of your student teacher. In order to observe effectively, a cooperating teacher needs to determine what recorded data will be most helpful to advance the growth of the student teacher at that point of professional development.

Data collections serve as opportunities to study and analyze what took place and reflect upon what that data tells your student teacher in regard to future decisions. The analysis of the *data* takes away the intimidation factor of the observation because it does not appear as an attempt to merely catch weaknesses. Instead the observation is recording evidence in a helpful way that will later be studied for professional direction and affirmation.

There are many different choices for the focus points of each data collection. There is value in using a variety throughout time and also occasionally returning to the same for comparison reasons. Suggestions for focus points can be derived from keying into these areas: teaching performance, the lesson development, and a reconstruction of the event.

The following are multiple ideas for you to consider when choosing topics for the many observations and data collections ahead. For observational purposes, it is better to choose one or two specific items from these areas for each observation rather than using any in entirety. Data collection on too many items at one time can overwhelm your student teacher and you as the collector of data.

Teacher Performance

Defining an effective teacher and components of successful instruction evoke an endless list of qualities and skills. The two examples below should provide and prompt you with plenty of options for focus points for data collections during formal observations.

In his *Student Teaching Performance Profile*, Sharpe (1969) identifies specific behaviors and a list of descriptors. Worthwhile data collections using any of these behaviors (or any of the partially listed descriptors) will be worth analyzing.

- Understanding and friendly
  Friendly, understanding, tactful, good-natured
  Shows concern for a pupil's personal needs
  Tolerant of errors on the part of pupils
  Finds good things in pupils and calls attention to them
  Listens encouragingly to pupils' viewpoints

- Planned and organized
  Presents evidence of thorough planning
  Objectives are clearly discernible
  Tells class what to expect during the period
  Has needed materials ready
  Keeps good records

- Stimulating and imaginative
  Original, encourages pupil initiative
  Presentations hold student interest
  Animated and enthusiastic
  Capitalizes on student interest

- Possesses self-confidence
  Sees self as liked, worthy, and able to do a good job
  Speaks confidently
  Poised in relations with students
  Takes mistakes and criticisms in stride
  Accepts new tasks readily

- Mastery of subject matter
  Recognizes important concepts and generalizations
  Focuses class presentations on basic concepts
  Relates to other fields
  Traces implications of knowledge

- Communicates well and empathetically
  Makes presentations at level of understanding
  Draws examples from interests of students
  Makes effective use of media
  Has no distracting mannerisms
  Speaks well

- Uses reasoning and creative thinking
  Seeks definition of problems
  Leads students to consider solutions
  Asks open-ended questions
  Encourages application of knowledge
  Encourages students to see the relationships among facts

- Directs attention to the logical operations in teaching
  Seeks definition of terms
  Encourages students to make inferences from information
  Demands examination of evidence
  Leads students to state assumptions
  Examines beliefs and opinions

Others have identified teaching skills in veteran teachers which should not be overlooked when observing your student teacher. For example, Danielson (2007) categorizes teaching into four specific domains. Although too extensive to present in this text, each of her four delineated domains provides common language for professional data collection and analysis with your student teacher.

- Domain 1: Planning and preparation
- Domain 2: The classroom environment
- Domain 3: Instruction
- Domain 4: Professional responsibilities

Finally, don't forget that your school district most likely has a teacher evaluation form. There are also many state teaching standards along with professional organizations that define teacher competencies, qualities, performance, responsibilities, and behaviors. These are easily accessed on the Internet. Examining these types of professional items offers other options for structuring a purposeful observation on teaching performance. Again, a narrow focus for collecting data is better than too general or too many items.

Lesson Framework

A second way of observing your student teacher is by watching what occurs within the framework of a particular lesson. This structures the observation specifically on instruction. One does not have to look far to find popular lesson plan formats to adopt for student teaching observational purposes. The observation can use parts or all of the lesson plan design. These are general elements found in most lesson formats:

- Climate for learning.
- Review.
- Preview of day's goal.
- Presentation of new material, ideas, skills.
- Check for learner understanding.
- Practice and drill.
- Assessment activities for new learning.

On the following pages are two forms which direct the focus of the observation on the framework of a lesson.

Lesson Analysis Form

Student Teacher:
Date & Time:
Grade & Subject:

Planning: lesson plan, materials, purposeful objective
Evidence:

Introduction: gains attention and interest, states objective
Evidence:

Strategies: effectiveness for content, learners, engagement, accommodations
Evidence:

Momentum: pacing, transitions, energy, movement, student participation
Evidence:

Delivery: voice, articulation, enthusiasm, vocabulary, grammar, nonverbals, pacing, clarity
Evidence:

Closure: summarization, content link to past or future learning
Evidence:

Classroom Climate: rapport, organization, management, discipline, student reaction
Evidence:

Assessment: check for understanding, questioning, practice, assessment piece(s), outcomes
Evidence:

Instructional Observation Checklist

Student Teacher:
Date & Time:
Grade & Subject:

	Yes	No	N/A
Were objectives and standards clearly identified?			
Were previously learned concepts and skills reviewed?			
Were students motivated at the opening and during the lesson?			
Was lesson sequenced appropriately?			
Was attention given to diverse learning styles and learner needs?			
Were students on task during the entire lesson?			
Were students actively involved in learning?			
Was transfer of learning built into the lesson?			
Was there evidence of monitoring comprehension during the lesson?			
Were students given an opportunity to practice or apply skills taught?			
Were directions clearly given?			
Was reinforcement used appropriately?			
Was assessment provided prior to the end of the lesson?			
Did the students appear to be correctly diagnosed?			
Were students given knowledge of results?			
If needed, were provisions made for re-teaching, extension, or retention?			
Did use of materials and activities facilitate the lesson?			
Did the teaching style fit the lesson?			
Were the lesson objectives and standards achieved?			
Comments:			

Event Reconstruction

Reconstruction is a data-gathering procedure that documents what happens as it happens. Later the documentation is analyzed to determine what prevails as the most important piece for you and your student teacher to address. There are endless ways to reconstruct the activities within a classroom. The following seven provide you with ideas for this method.

Scripting

Scripting is the recording of every person, event, or item that attracts the attention of the observer. You record only what you see or hear. The intent is to be descriptive and not evaluative so the narrative should contain an objective summary of your student teacher's class activity.

With practice the observer can write quickly enough to keep up with the flow of events. Others resort to a list of phrases rather than sentences. It is impossible to record all that occurs in a classroom but scripting can provide a strong silhouette for analysis.

Categorical Frequency Instruments

A categorical frequency instrument isolates an aspect of teaching. Behaviors and actions on that aspect are documented during the observation and then tabulated for analysis. For example, if you want to focus an observation on questioning, you would devise a chart that records the number and the types of questions during a lesson or time period. You might even record the wording of each question to analyze later.

Recordings

Through the use of audio and visual technology, you can watch and listen to a recording of how the learners and student teacher interact when you are not in the room. Your student teacher can also use the recording to self-evaluate. Another option is for both of you to view or listen to a recording together to generate analysis.

Teacher Classroom Activity Profile

Sharpe's (1969) study of student teachers categorized seven classroom activities. Using these categories (a worksheet follows), the observer records the activity in three-minute intervals. The data will show how a teacher spends time, the types of intellectual activity stressed, the number of activities, and the types of interruption that occur. Of course, you can change the categories to collect different data for analysis.

Teacher Classroom Activity Profile

Time																			Summary	
	1	2	3	4	5	6	7	8	9	10	11	12	13	14	15	16	17	18	Min.	%
Teacher activity																				
Management: nonlearning																				
Management: learning																				
Random discussion																				
Presentation																				
Recitational drill																				
Logical thinking																				
Thinking process																				
Explanatory Notes Comments																				

TEACHER:
CLASS:
DATE:
OBSERVER:

Visual Diagramming

Visual diagramming is a method of capturing behavior through the construction of a diagram that visually illustrates a pattern of activity during the lesson. For example, to record class participation during discussions you might draw a seating chart. Using tally marks, you record on the chart which learner responds to questions from the student teacher and to peer comments.

Another example is to graph the pattern of your student teacher's movement throughout the classroom during the lesson presentation. Using a classroom diagram, you draw and then later analyze the movement of your student teacher and what that means to teaching and learning.

Student Evaluation

Examining learners' tests and homework can provide interesting insights into your student teacher's teaching abilities. Analyzing the evaluation piece provides your student teacher with data to determine if different instructional approaches or assessment instruments would have been more appropriate for the learners. Additionally, it provides another opportunity for a student teacher to gain a different concept of student comprehension and capabilities. Areas in which the cooperating teacher will want to collect data when viewing the evaluation piece are:

- ☐ *Content.* What indicates the piece adequately represent the content taught? From where have ideas been obtained in the development of this piece (manual, Internet, resource books, campus courses)?

- ☐ *Accountability.* What indicates that standards are met? What accommodations are needed and addressed? Is this evaluation tied to the report card? Is there an appropriate total number of points for the test? What grading scale is used?

- ☐ *Construction.* When have learners had similar engagements required in this piece? Is the set-up appealing and user-friendly? Are spelling, punctuation, and grammar correct? Is the vocabulary grade-level appropriate? Are directions clear? What types of questions are used? How many of each type of question are present? What is the point value for each type of question? If performance based, what criteria and rubrics are used? What is the anticipated time for students to complete this piece?

- ☐ *Outcome of the evaluation piece.* How did students score on the piece? How long did it take students to complete the piece? Were there any clarifying questions asked by students? Were there any student comments about the piece? How would you describe the testing environment?

Written Communication

Written communication is a widely used and professionally acceptable supervisory tool (Bolin, 1988) and supplements the more traditional oral method. This interplay of ideas can become a dialogue where you and your student teacher exchange views and information in writing, often when conversation is not possible such as when one or the other is teaching or out of the room. Written communication can achieve the following functions:

Provides a record of progress
- Immediate reaction to performance
- Suggestions for improvements
- Indications of why a lesson was well-taught
- Encouragement to the student teacher

Compiles a number of useful teaching ideas
- List of ways to manage specific teaching problems
- List of ways to cope with difficult students
- Ideas for providing variety in the classroom
- Sources of instructional materials and aids

Gives written confirmation of agreements
- Definition of responsibilities
- Clarification of verbal agreements
- Location for resources and items
- Exchange of questions and answers
- Documentation of reminders

Encourages reflection
- Examination of ideas and practices
- Probe for the student teacher to think about teaching

Provides a record of professional information
- School procedures and regulations
- Professional information about students
- Exchange of resources including people and web sources

A notebook makes a durable form for written conversation. A middle line may be drawn to serve as a dividing line for the responses of the two participants. Examples of written communication initiated by both parties party are illustrated on the next page.

Examples of Written Communication

October	4
When do you want the new bulletin board displayed?	Monday is fine.
The students gave little response to my questions. Why?	Try to be more specific because questions such as "How about roots?" are hard for student to know what you had in mind for an answer.
What did you think of the unit introduction? Yes, this was a surprise to me! I know how to better plan now. Okay, I will review. Can we talk more about ways to review in a quick, fun way later today?	You did this well. The students remained attentive. Word usage was at an appropriate level and you coordinated the events nicely. Did you notice that students needed more time to get papers and pencil ready? When there is time remaining as there was today, use it for review or for explaining the assignment. We'll have time to talk between class periods.
Simon acted strangely today. Do you know what is going on? No. I will finish on Friday.	He is being treated for manic-depression syndrome. He may not have taken his medication. Let's watch him closely today. Have you had time to read through all of the student files yet?
Paul is not making any progress. I wonder if this classroom is the right place for him.	In spite of poor academic work, he is acquiring attitudes, values, and friendships. This is a part of educating too.
I liked the method that you used to choose which student should answer your questions. I am going to try it in my next lesson.	I'll watch for it! Remind me to show you the website where I found the idea.
Thanks for your tips and reminders! Student Council is holding a bake sale in the cafeteria so I'll buy some dessert for us!	1. Get attendance out by 8:15. 2. Close the door when hallway noise occurs. 3. Save time by letting the kids help you pass out materials. 4. Don't forget we have a meeting over lunch tomorrow to review your case study progress. I'll bring salads for us.

LEAVING THE CLASSROOM

As time progresses, you may wonder if you should remain in the class-room at all times. Check with your student teacher's college to see if guidance is offered on this issue. A student teacher needs to be alone with the students in the class often enough to feel a personal responsibility for what happens and to develop confidence in working independently. On the other hand, you must be in the room enough to observe the teaching style of the student teacher for analytical and evaluative purposes and to keep abreast of what is happening in the classroom with your learners, for whom you ultimately hold responsibility.

Unfortunately, two detrimental patterns may develop. The first, and perhaps the most damaging, is when a cooperating teacher chooses to allow a student teacher to be alone with the class too early or too often. This prevents the opportunity for the cooperating teacher to observe dif-ficulties or to reinforce good teaching behaviors. In essence, this places the student teacher in a risky trial-and-error predicament.

The other pattern is one in which a cooperating teacher almost never leaves the room while a student teacher is teaching. In this case the stu-dent teacher does not have a chance to establish a teacher-pupil relation-ship because the cooperating teacher will be the dominant person. It may cause the student teacher to be uneasy and to feel every move must be monitored. It simply smothers growth, confidence, and independence.

The amount of informal and formal observation time has to be care-fully determined and is affected by the amount of time that you are in the classroom. Although it is highly recommended that you be present in the classroom the majority of time, once your student teacher exhibits consis-tent competencies, consider incorporating the following progression with each set of students and for each content area:

1. Be in and out of the classroom briefly during some lessons.
2. Observe the first part of a lesson and then leave for the second part.
3. Leave for the first half and then observe during the second half of a lesson.
4. Observe for an entire lesson one day and be absent for that content lesson the next day.
5. During the late stages of student teaching, occasionally leave for longer blocks of times, such as half of the morning one day, half of the afternoon another day.
6. Leave for one full morning and another day leave for one full after-noon.
7. Leave the student teacher alone for one entire day, but this should be done at the ending stage of the experience.

You should only leave when you are convinced that the student teacher is capable. The student teacher should know at all times where the cooperating teacher can be reached within the school in case of problems.

In summary, all observations when accompanied by data collection provide beneficial information. Your coaching position as an observer of your student teacher is a crucial one since the data you collect will be used in the conference to document and facilitate the growth of your student teacher.

Note to Self:
- ✓ Conferences use data to focus on improving teaching & learning.
- ✓ Through conferencing, CTs coach STs to reflect.
- ✓ Communication includes words & body language.
- ✓ Different abstraction & commitment levels require different supervisory approaches.
- ✓
- ✓

Chapter 4

What Do I Say During a Conference?

The conferences that follow observations are rich opportunities for your student teacher's professional growth. Imagine the valuable discussions that can occur after your student teacher observes you or someone else teaching and after you observe your student teacher teaching. Effective conferences interpret what happened and prod future action.

Conferences range from the informal to the formal. A complete program will incorporate both. It is because of your coaching throughout many conferences that your student teacher evolves into a reflective practitioner.

Informal conferences are held as needed and keep the lines of communication open. These brief, casual, and often spontaneous meetings allow for immediate feedback, help to establish rapport, relieve tension, and provide quick fixes and general information. If you and your student teacher are accustomed to continuous informal interaction, the comfort level carries over to the formal setting.

In contrast to informal conferences, formal conferences have specific purposes and focus more deeply on the professional development of the student teacher. These sessions should be scheduled for a specific time and place and include a planned agenda of topics that relate to the development of teaching competence. They should occur soon after the formal observations. A typical agenda includes this checklist of topics:

☐ Progress on topics and goals since last conference

☐ Analysis of teaching behaviors using new data

☐ Discussion of strengths

☐ Planning future course of actions and goals for growth

☐ Information about the school and students

☐ Questions and concerns from the student teacher

Conferences should be a normal, consistent staple of the student-teaching experience. The more often conferences are held, the more comfortable the cooperating teacher becomes with their supervisory coaching role and the student teacher becomes more comfortable with the conference procedure as a positive vehicle for professional growth.

EFFECTIVE COMMUNICATION

A successful conference depends on the ability to communicate. Talking can be futile if there is no comprehension or acceptance by the other participant. O'Shea, Hoover, and Carroll (1988) as well as Talvitie, Peltokallio, and Mannisto (2000) report that a lack of communication accounts for many student teaching problems. In a survey of over three hundred student teachers, Connor and Killmer (1995) find that cooperating teachers are judged effective when they communicate and provide appropriate feedback to their charges. So it is clear that the cooperating teacher needs to develop and refine communication skills in order to make the conference successful. The points below guide you in this necessary supervisory skill.

Frame of Reference

Becoming adept with communication for the sake of a successful conference begins with an understanding of a frame of reference for your student teacher. Glickman (1981; 1995) proposes that different supervisory approaches with classroom teachers should be taken depending upon the level of development of the person being supervised. Henry (1995) applies Glickman's ideas to the specific process of supervising student teachers. The frame of reference for your student teacher begins with identifying the levels of commitment and abstraction.

Student teachers vary in their *level of commitment*. At low levels, they appear to be indifferent and perhaps even lazy. They may resort to lecturing and asking low-level questions. They are inclined to be satisfied with minimum standards only and have less commitment to the profession.

At the other end of the continuum are student teachers with a high level of commitment. These student teachers are committed to the learners they teach and are eager to make their teaching more effective. They are normally high-energy people who plan to make a career in teaching.

The other variable to determine is the *level of abstraction*. This refers to the student teacher's ability to conceptualize and draw alternatives or options from knowledge, skills, and resources. At a low level of abstraction, student teachers may think in concrete terms and stereotype students, seeing no more than one alternative to a problem or blaming problems on external forces.

Student teachers with a high level of abstraction are more able to differentiate and integrate. They see alternatives to addressing a question or a teaching problem. They will more likely take risks, explore ideas, and encourage learners to be creative. They see that differences exist among learners and use a variety of teaching models.

When combining commitment and abstraction levels, four distinct quadrants surface. The quadrants can be used for identifying your student teacher at any particular time and in any particular situation. The level of commitment and abstraction are not the same in every situation, nor do they remain the same overtime. What levels of commitment and abstraction are demonstrated by your student teacher in the situation you wish to analyze?

	Quad 1	Quad 2	Quad 3	Quad 4
Low Abstraction	✔	✔		
High Abstraction			✔	✔
Low Commitment	✔		✔	
High Commitment		✔		✔

- *Quadrant 1: Low abstraction, Low commitment.* This student teacher has difficulty defining problems and knows fewer ways of addressing them. She usually thinks in concrete terms, where there is only one solution or an easy answer to a problem. She categorizes pupils rather than considering them to be unique. She will likely be unimaginative and teach in a style that requires the least amount of preparation. She is often one of the first people leaving the school at the end of the day.
- *Quadrant 2: Low abstraction, High commitment.* This student teacher may be eager but lack a sense of direction. High on commitment, he will devote an endless amount of energy to the job but this energy will likely not be coupled with a definable purpose. The problem is not desire; it is a lack of abstraction. If he has an idea, he lacks the ability to bring it to fruition or to discriminate if it will work and or not.
- *Quadrant 3: High abstraction, Low commitment.* This student teacher will be intelligent, but have a lesser concern for teaching. He may verbalize what can or should be done but does not follow through. Because of low motivation, progress toward acceptable levels of teacher competency is slow to develop or is virtually nonexistent. He is a thinker but not a doer.
- *Quadrant 4: High abstraction, High commitment.* This student teacher demonstrates high intellectual capacity, sees pupils as unique individuals, is aware of alternative teaching strategies, and is willing to try techniques that involve some risks. This person is enthusiastic about, and dedicated to, the teaching profession.

Supervisory Styles for Different Quadrants

Once you identify the quadrant of your student teacher in the situation that you are analyzing, you can use that knowledge for determining the best supervisory approach to use during the conference. Again, Henry (1995) specifically applies Glickman's research on supervising teachers to the process of supervising student teachers in each of the following quadrants.

Quadrant 1 = Directive Control

The Quadrant 1 student teacher needs to be motivated and informed. In this situation you can assume that she needs a structured environment. The supervisory approach most likely to succeed is a directive-control model, in which the cooperating teacher gives specific instructions and standardizes expectations. You tell the student teacher what should be done and describe the indicators for success. For example, a cooperating teacher might say, "John, I want you to spend fifteen minutes in class tomorrow questioning students about their understanding of the assignment and have them draw conclusions about its relationship to the previous unit. Page 52 in the manual should give you some ideas for thoughtful questions."

Quadrant 2 = Directive Informational

The Quadrant 2 student teacher responds well with a type of directive supervision in which information is the key. You provide ideas to increase the abstraction level and allow your student teacher to make the decision from those choices. A cooperating teacher may say, "You can have students demonstrate their ideas by creating a poster, working in groups to explore each other's ideas, or presenting case studies. Which do you want to use?" In this case you would be filling in the vacuum of low abstraction ability by providing ideas. The highly motivated student teacher would then be willing to make a choice and spend the energy to see that the activities are accomplished.

Quadrant 3 = Collaborative

The Quadrant 3 student teachers can define a problem and think through possible solutions. Let your student teacher offer ideas and you can add more if necessary. The suggestions can be examined in a collaborative manner and the decision can be mutually determined. Since the commitment is weak, both parties will agree on a course of action. A cooperating teacher might say, "I like your ideas for the science experiment. There are some materials that are found in the media lab that you can explore after lunch. When can we test the experiment tomorrow?"

Quadrant 4 = Indirect

The best style of supervision for this student teacher is an indirect approach. Since the student teacher can generate a variety of alternative plans and is dedicated to implementation, your role is one of support and encouragement. Appropriate questions might be "Have you thought about something really different and exciting to introduce the next unit?" or "I like your use of centers. How can you use them for other content areas?" Through questions, probing, and interest, you encourage your student teacher to be more purposeful, creative, and reflective.

The following visual highlights the prior explanations of the frame of reference of student teachers and the corresponding supervisory approaches for cooperating teachers. It also provides you with some potential communication prompts to use during conferences to achieve the intended outcome for your student teacher (Weber 2014).

Quadrant	Cooperating Teacher	Student Teacher
1 ↓AC	Directive Control: Inform, direct, motivate *Let me provide some ideas on how this can unfold. Did you catch all the details? What questions do you have?*	Listen, take action as defined, expand awareness of teaching and learning
2 ↓A ↑C	Informational: Suggest options, provide information, give choice *Do you have some ideas? Have you considered__? Which of these ideas do you think will work? What resources do you need? This book is a resource of ideas.*	Listen for details and choices, make selection for action, expand repertoire
3 ↑A ↓C	Collaborative: Negotiate solutions and follow through *What are ways that this can be approached? How do you think the pupils will react? When will it be ready? Summarize our plan.*	Collaborate, verbalize decisions, meet timeline
4 ↑AC	Indirect: Affirm, coach, push to think *What do you think? Why? What if that doesn't work? I like that you___. Explain your choice.*	Analyze, problem-solve

If you understand and employ the ever-important communication skills for supervision, you are well on your way to maximizing the conference with your student teacher. However, there are still other points in regard to conducting conferences that need to have your supervisory attention.

POSITIVE RAPPORT

Good interpersonal relationships must be established between you and your student teacher. A conference is dominated by data, but the success of a conference depends upon the affective climate of the discussion as well. An effective conference models good human relations and an attitude of mutual trust and respect.

As the cooperating teacher, you set the conference tone, so you must be conscious of factors that help to create rapport. The possibilities are numerous but the following are a helpful start for establishing positive rapport with your student teacher:

- *Be an empathetic person.* You may not accept or change what a student teacher believes, but show empathy. Respond to the student through verbal and nonverbal behaviors to show that you understand how she feels.
- *Choose words carefully.* A poor choice of words or an ill-chosen expression can create unnecessary tension or alienation.
- *Be a good listener.* Indicate that you are aware of what is being said. Do not get so preoccupied formulating responses that you fail to really listen.
- *Exhibit supportive nonverbal behavior.* Body language is more believable than oral statements. Facial expressions, gestures, voice tone, and other kinetic behavior matter.
- *Respond to the needs expressed by the student teacher.* Work with the student teacher to solve problems and to satisfy concerns.
- *Maintain objectivity.* Emphasis should be placed on what was said and done, rather than on opinions of what occurred. Look for the facts and try not to be influenced emotionally.

HABIT OF REFLECTION

Corcoran and Leahy (2003) suggest that developing the habit of reflection as a student teacher carries into the teaching career. Reflection is a necessary tool for facing the demands and challenges of the teaching profession. You need to help your student teachers develop this skill so that it becomes a habit.

Self-analysis should be encouraged throughout conferences because it is one of the most effective ways to produce change. This allows a student teacher to solve problems through discovery instead of listening. S. O'Neal's research (1983) is a strong reminder that your student teacher will become more involved with your encouragement.

One of the best ways of encouraging self-appraisal is through questioning. Pultorak (1993) presents a taxonomy of questions that lead to reflective analysis. Consider how each of them might help your student teacher be more reflective.

- What were essential strengths of the lesson?
- What, if anything, would you change about the lesson?
- Do you think the lesson was successful? Why?
- Which conditions were important to the outcome?
- What, if any, unanticipated learning outcomes resulted from the lesson?
- Can you think of another way you might have taught this lesson?
- Can you think of alternative pedagogical approaches to teaching this lesson that might improve the learning process?
- Do you think the content covered was important to students? Why?
- Did any moral or ethical concerns occur as a result of the lesson?

THE RIGHT FOCUS

The right focus for conferences centers on the improvement of teaching and learning. The data collection opens conversation for this purpose. By analyzing, reflecting upon, and discussing the data, the conferences recognize strengths and areas in need of strengthening. Spotlighting the data and what it reveals about teaching and learning takes the student teacher's focus off herself and moves it to the students. A focus on data also lessens the subjectivity of the cooperating teacher.

On a related note, the location of your conference influences the amount of focus given to the overall conference. Choose a location where interruptions are minimal and privacy is assured. An empty classroom or office, or a private corner in the library works better than the teacher's lounge or hallway. Each of you should feel comfortable in speaking without being overheard by others and also in knowing that the time set aside for the conference is a priority.

STUDY OF RESULTS

As you are now aware, holding an effective conference with your student teacher takes thoughtful planning and execution. Your skills and confidence will develop over time. To determine whether a conference was successful, use the following form or use the checklist.

Conference Analysis

Quadrant Level of Student Teacher: (Circle) 1 2 3 4	**ST Plan of Action:**
Date of Conference:	
Location of Conference:	
Method of Data Collection:	**Plan determined by:** (Circle one) Student Teacher Cooperating Teacher Collaboratively
Topics for Conference Based on Data:	**Questions/Topics Posed by Student Teacher:**
Questions to Encourage ST Reflection on above:	
Strengths to Mention:	**Estimated Percentage of Conference Time:** ___% Data Analysis & Plan Development ___% Reflection ___% Information ___% Cooperating Teacher Talk ___% Student Teacher Talk
Other Agenda Items (unrelated to observation):	**Follow-up items:**

Conference Checklist:

- ☐ Does the student teacher show evidence of having new ideas?
- ☐ Does the student teacher bring up problems?
- ☐ Is there free and clear communication?
- ☐ Is there observable evidence to document the suggestions?
- ☐ Are the suggestions linked to the impact on the pupils?
- ☐ Will the suggestions be carried out?
- ☐ Is the student teacher learning to evaluate herself objectively?
- ☐ Was there adequate time for both cooperating teacher and student teacher input?

An effective conference contains serious dialogue in a supportive environment. Using the data, you coach your student teacher in reflecting upon what worked and what needs to be addressed to strengthen future teaching and learning. The conference is a crucial instructional time for your student teacher. Whether the conference occurs after you observe your student teacher or after your student teacher collects data from observing someone, each conference should be approached in a positive, helpful manner to maximize the growth of the future teacher.

Chapter 5

Should My Student Teacher Be Involved Beyond My Classroom?

It takes time to plan for and run an effective classroom. Also a typical teacher usually attends professional meetings throughout the work day, leads student extracurricular activities, takes on extra duties for managing the school, and makes time to attend evening and weekend school events.

Due to your student teacher's inexperience, you may wonder how wise it is to involve her in other parts of the total school program. If student teaching is to provide an opportunity for a comprehensive overview of teaching, then it makes sense to facilitate your student teacher's participation in school-related activities, duties, meetings, and events. However, while an enriching opportunity for a student teacher, the timing, amount, and level of participation must be tempered with the priority given to learning to be an effective classroom instructor.

BENEFITS OF PARTICIPATION

The time and energy spent in out-of-the-classroom participation is a good investment for a student teacher. Worthwhile participation will make important contributions to the overall development of a student teacher in multiple ways. Your student teacher will benefit by:

- Getting to know and understand pupils better.
- Understanding the types of learning that occur outside the classroom.
- Becoming more aware of the demands that are made on a teacher.
- Meeting and interacting with parents and other adults in the community.
- Working alongside other teachers.
- Enhancing her visibility to school and community members.
- Learning about the purposes and functions of the school.
- Understanding how forces work together for the education of pupils.
- Making contribution to the students, staff, and school.
- Exhibiting other personal and professional dimensions.

TYPES OF PARTICIPATION

Does your student teacher know how and when teachers participate outside of their classroom? Speak with him about teacher duties involving recess, cafeteria, and bus schedules. Explain the professional meetings that take place during and outside of school hours such as meetings for grade level, content, diagnostic purposes, planning, and fund-raising. Your student teacher will be aware of teacher involvement in the coaching of sports, but do they know about the ancillary positions plus all the other student organizations that have teacher sponsors?

The range of activities and duties is extensive. Obviously a student teacher will not be able to see and do everything so priorities will need to be determined. Although there is no one pattern of specific activities that is appropriate to all situations, the following list represents those experiences where student teachers can usually be involved:

- Faculty Duties
  Attendance at school board meetings
  Hall, bus, playground, cafeteria, and detention supervision
  Coordination of aides and volunteers
  Reports and other required information
  Parent conferences
  Attendance at school functions
  After-school assistance to learners
  Rehearsals and practices
  Conferences regarding learners
  Field trips

- Professional Activities
  Faculty and district meetings
  Inservice programs
  Grant writing
  Textbook and technology selection
  Committee assignments
  Professional meetings and conferences
  Professional organization activities

- Extracurricular Functions
  Athletic contests
  Drama activities
  Musical events
  Fund-raisers
  Student clubs
  Student government
  Student social activities
  Academic competitions

- Other
  Faculty functions
  Community functions

You may wish to record the ways in which your student teacher participates in the total school program. The general rule of thumb is to include your student teacher in all faculty meetings and the duties of the cooperating teacher. Provide some isolated experiences from both the professional activities and extracurricular functions to help give your student teacher a feel for additional types of opportunities available. Use the worksheet to track your student teacher's participation over the course of the student teaching experience.

Participation Activities for Student Teachers

1. Supervisory Duties during the School Hours, Other than Instruction

2. Professional Teacher Meetings

3. School Social Activities

4. Teacher Social Activities

5. Student Athletic Activities

6. Student Clubs and Organizations

7. School-Wide Events

8. Fund-Raising Events

9. Communication with Parents

10. Community-Related Functions

FACILITATION OF PARTICIPATION

As you direct the participation of your student teacher, care must be taken not to distract him from the time needed to develop effective teaching skills. Some types of participation are firmly linked to classroom instruction and are appropriate to be required. Others are divergent opportunities whose value of participation must be weighed against the teaching demands of the student teacher. While all student teachers need the opportunity to experience out-of-class participation, the timing of the experience and the competency level of the student teacher will determine the amount. Effective instruction is the foremost priority of student teaching.

Of special cautions are those exuberant student teachers who over-volunteer and the hesitant ones who feel pressure to oblige a veteran teacher but truly need time for teaching preparations. Even though extra hands or current expertise are helpful in out-of-classroom settings, you must kindly counsel or intervene to moderate an appropriate amount of participation for your student teacher.

The world beyond the classroom may not be as readily apparent to the student teacher. Your student teacher needs to be made aware of the obligations associated with successful participation. The checklist below may be of assistance for this task:

- [ ] Determine a student teacher's interests to see how they can be incorporated into the existing activity, duty, meeting, or event.
- [ ] Describe a typical pattern of teacher obligations for each out-of-class activity, duty, meeting, and event.
- [ ] Explain what is expected from a student teacher who participates.
- [ ] Invite your student teacher to accompany you (or others) in the duties of the role.
- [ ] Provide literature on the subject or needed materials when appropriate.
- [ ] Explain what student teachers can learn from participation.
- [ ] Inform the student teacher about related policies and protocols.
- [ ] Discuss ways to balance the teaching load with participation.

To enhance the experience further, follow up with a reflective discussion about the activity, duty, meeting, and event.

- [ ] How did you perform in your role?
- [ ] What did you learn from this experience?

☐ What did you learn by observing other adult participants?

☐ How will this make you a stronger classroom teacher?

☐ Is this activity one which you wish to continue?

For years, many states have embraced the principles identified by the Interstate New Teacher Assessment and Support Consortium (1992) as competencies that beginning teachers should possess before a teaching license is issued. Principle ten of that document states the following performance criteria: "The teacher fosters relationships with school colleagues, parents, and agencies in the larger community to support students' learning and well-being." This initiative adds incentive for you to give serious time and effort to overseeing the participation activities of your student teacher.

Your supervisory coaching responsibility is one of informing and guiding. This involves making certain that your student teacher is aware of the out-of-classroom time that consumes a teacher's day and arranging for participation in appropriate activities, duties, meetings, and events. In addition, each opportunity becomes an important topic for reflective conversation between you and your student teacher.

Epilogue

Being a cooperating teacher is a rewarding yet complex role which you should undertake with confidence and clear direction. This is the second of the "little instruction books that should come with your student teacher" to assist you in your supervisory role. It guides you in the foundation for observations, conferences, and the supervision of lesson plans and school-related experiences during the student-teaching experience. As you are now well aware, coaching is the most demanding and crucial supervisory element for building an effective beginning teacher.

You may wonder if there is more to the cooperating teacher role than the preparation (book 1) and coaching (book 2). Definitely! Significant problems may surface, and the conclusion of the experience means there will be an evaluation to complete and a letter of recommendation to write.

We will be there to help guide you through more of those what-do-I-do-now moments during the final stage of your cooperating teacher role. We hope that you'll journey with us through *Evaluating a Student Teacher* (book 3), which is the last book of *Student Teaching: The Cooperating Teacher Series*.

Ann and Marvin

What Would You Do? You can practice your supervisory skill using real-life situations. Access Book 2 student teaching case studies at https://rowman.com/WebDocs/Bk2CaseStudies_coachonline.pdf

---

References

Anderson, J. B., and J. H. Freiberg (1995). Using self-assessment as a reflective tool to enhance the student teaching experience. *Teacher Education Quarterly* 22(1): 77–91.

Bolin, F. S. (1988). Helping student teachers think about teaching. *Journal of Teacher Education* 39(2): 48–54.

Conner, K., and N. Killmer (1995). *Evaluation of cooperating teacher effectiveness.* Retrieved from ERIC database. (ED394950).

Corcoran, C. A., and R. Leahy (2003). Growing professionally through reflective practice. *Kappa Delta Pi Record* 40(1): 30–33.

Danielson, C. (2007). *Enhancing professional practice: A framework for teaching.* Alexandria, VA: Association for School Curriculum and Development.

Fleming, L. C., and P. H. Baker (2002). *Differentiating in the classroom: A study of student teachers.* Retrieved from ERIC database. (ED479480).

Giebelhaus, C. (1995). *Revisiting a step-child: Supervision in teacher education.* Retrieved from ERIC database. (ED391785).

Glickman, C. D. (1995). *Supervision of instruction: A developmental approach.* Newton, MA: Allyn & Bacon.

——— (1981). *Developmental supervision: Alternative practices for helping teachers improve instruction.* Alexandria, VA: Association for Supervision and Curriculum Development.

Grove, K., N. Strudler, and S. Odell (2004). Mentoring toward technology use: Cooperating teacher practice in supporting student teachers. *Journal of Research on Technology in Education* 37(1): 85–109.

Guyton, E., and J. McIntyre (1990). Student teaching and school experiences. In *Handbook of research on teacher education,* edited by W. R. Houston, 514–34. New York: Macmillan.

Hawkey, K. (1995). Learning from peers: The experience of student teachers in school-based teacher education. *Journal of Teacher Education* 46(3): 175–83.

Henry, M. A. (1995). Supervising student teachers: A new paradigm. In *Making the difference for teachers: The field experience in actual practice,* edited by G. A. Slick. Thousand Oaks, CA: Corwin Press.

Interstate New Teacher Assessment and Support Consortium (1992). *Model standards for beginning teacher licensing, assessment and development: A resource for state dialogue.* Retrieved August 3, 2015, from http://www.ccsso.org/content/pdfs/corestrd.pdf.

O'Neal, S. (1983). *An analysis of student teaching-cooperating teacher conferences as related to the self-concept, flexibility, and teaching concerns of each participant.* Retrieved from ERIC database. (ED234030).

O'Neal, S. F. (1983). *Developing effective instructional planning and decision-making skills: Are we training teachers or technicians?* Retrieved from ERIC database. (ED240105).

O'Shea, L. J., N. L. Hoover, and R. G. Carroll (1988). Effective intern conferencing. *Journal of Teacher Education* 39(2): 17–21.

Pultorak, E. G. (1993). Facilitating reflective thought in novice teachers. *Journal of Teacher Education* 44(4): 288–95.

Rauch, K., and C. R. Whitaker (1999). Observation and feedback during student teaching: Learning from peers. *Action in Teacher Education* 21(3): 67–78.

Sharpe, D. M. (1969). *Isolating relevant variables in student teacher assessment.* Retrieved from ERIC database. (ED028999).

Talvitie, U., L. Peltokallio, and P. Mannisto (2000). Student teachers' views about their relationships with university supervisors, cooperating teachers, and peer student teachers. *Scandinavian Journal of Educational Research* 44(1): 79–88.

Treiber, F. (1984). Ineffective teaching: Can we learn from it? *Journal of Teacher Education* 35(5): 45–46.

Weber, A. (2014, June). *Three: A perfect number.* Presentations at the New Jersey Teacher Partnership for Mentor Preparation's Cooperating Teachers' Institute, Union City and Tom's River, NJ.

About the Authors

Marvin A. Henry served as professor of education and chairperson of curriculum and instruction at Indiana State University where he was also a supervisor of student teachers and field director for student teaching. He is a former president and a distinguished member of the Association of Teacher Educators as well as a recipient of its Outstanding Program in Teacher Education award.

Ann Weber served as instructional assistant professor in teacher education at Illinois State University. She collaborated with cooperating teachers while supervising hundreds of student teachers and was also the innovator in developing and teaching an online course in the supervision of student teachers.

The authors' experience, research, and passion in teacher education span over fifty-five years! They co-authored *Supervising Student Teachers the Professional Way*, seventh edition, which is a more extensive treatment of supervisory responsibilities, and its instructor's guide. They continue as speakers, writers, and advocates for the professional development of cooperating teachers. Authors can be reached at SSTTPW@gmail.com.